Kindertransport, Before and After:

Elegy and Celebration

*

Sixty Poems 1980-2007

by

Lotte Kramer

`Weep for his passing,
Sing for his living, ...`
(`For Friedrich Sandels`)

Edited with an Introduction by

Sybil Oldfield

Centre for German Jewish Studies, University of Sussex

This paperback ed. published in 2007 by the Centre for German Jewish
Studies, University of Sussex.

British Library Cataloguing-in-Publication Data
A catalogue record for this book is available from the British Library

ISBN 978-0-9554114-2-7

Cover design by Keith Hunt, University of Sussex Print and
Reprographic Unit

Printed and bound in Great Britain

Cover photo: Jewish refugee children at UK customs; Wiener Library,
London.

Book orders: £10.00 plus £2.50 p&p from either:

Centre for German Jewish Studies, Arts B, University of Sussex,
Brighton, BN1 9QN
Or
Sybil Oldfield, 4 Houndean Close, Lewes, East Sussex, BN7 1EZ

CONTENTS

Acknowledgments

Acknowledgements are due to the publishers of Lotte Kramer's earlier collections:
Annakin Press, Poet and Printer, Hippopotamus Press and Rockingham Press.

We are also grateful to Alisa Franklin for transcribing the poems on to disk and to Vicky East, Keith Hunt and Will Barker of the University of Sussex Print and Reprographic Unit.

Sophie Cahn (1880-1964), Lotte Kramer's English teacher in Mainz and rescuer. A gifted musician as well as an inspiring language teacher and lover of literature, she introduced Lotte to the work of Rilke. Exiled from her world of German education and culture, Sophie Cahn found herself in the English countryside in wartime, trying without success to raise rabbits and pigs. Eventually she and Mrs. Fyleman (see Introduction) attempted the boarding and rehabilitation of juvenile delinquent girls - not an easy undertaking (see `The House` in Lotte Kramer's The Phantom Lane, 2000). Intensely intellectually alive as well as intensely warm-hearted, she had a special gift for communicating with children and became foster grandmother to Lotte's son. All her pupils in Germany, Jewish or not, were enriched by her and the city of Mainz now has a *Sophie Cahnstrasse* in her honour. Lotte grieved that her teacher never knew she would become a published poet – but Sophie Cahn bequeathed to her all her first editions of Rilke, so perhaps she guessed.

Introduction

Lotte Kramer was fifteen when she escaped on one of the last *Kindertransport* trains from Mainz – a city with a thousand years of Jewish habitation - in July 1939. It would be nearly another forty years before she began to write about her past. She is still writing.

Her father, Ernst Wertheimer, had been a playwright before the First World War, a war in which he himself had been wounded and his brother awarded the Iron Cross for valour. After 1919 he had joined his young wife's family business, a wine and liqueur factory in Mainz, but still wrote unpublished, unproduced scripts, shut away in his desk. Her `gentle mother` Sofie, (see `WAVING`), concentrated on looking after the home and their only child. Lotte enjoyed a happy, protected, Liberal Jewish German middle-class childhood, surrounded by a large extended family and many friends - including non-Jews. She attended the ordinary Volksschule until she was eleven in 1934, joining, like all her little schoolmates – 50 in the class, 10 Jewish, 40 not – in round-eyed, pitying veneration for the young martyr Horst Wessel and in lusty singing of the new, catchy, patriotic songs. Her parents, after 1933, successfully sheltered their daughter from whatever political anxiety they felt themselves. And the compulsorily Jewish-only Secondary School turned out to be a very positive experience for Lotte because some of the most gifted teachers in the whole city, having been forbidden to teach non-Jewish children in the *Gymnasien* of Mainz, were now her charismatic teachers of German literature, English, Science, Music.

Then came brutal *Kristallnacht.* 9/10 November 1938 hit her as a traumatic shock; suddenly she realized for the first time that she would have to leave her home and country. There was not much discussion in her family, simply the acceptance of the leadership of Lotte's English teacher Sophie Cahn, who would not get out of Germany herself unless she could take a group of young people to escape with her. It was Sophie Cahn who negotiated, with the help of Quakers in Germany and in Britain, both the necessary financial sponsorship and places on the *Kindertransport* train for five girls including Lotte. And it was she who found the essential `hostess` in Britain willing to take into her home a middle-aged Jewish teacher plus her five adolescent pupils. [1]

Lotte's mother packed and repacked the suitcase. The parting at the railway station was terrible, her mother crying uncontrollably while Lotte cried to see her cry. Once on the train, however, there was an irrepressible feeling among the girls of release, exhilaration, adventure. Not one of them, of course, dreamed that the parting had been for ever.

And the arrival?

Lotte found herself, her teacher, her friends, living in an amazing *ménage*, Fendley House near Tring in Hertfordshire. Margaret Fyleman, the lady of the house, was an eccentric, cultured Irishwoman (married to a retired Indian Civil Servant). She had studied singing in Berlin before 1914 and had very happy memories of the life there, including many German Jewish friends. One of Mrs. Fyleman's daughters was an actress who brought home more cosmopolitan refugees – her artistic friends from London. Sometimes twenty people would sit down to dinner, after which there would be the singing of Schubert *Lieder* (accompanied on the piano by Sophie Cahn), or play-readings, or J.B.Priestley's broadcast talks on the BBC, or the recital of Shakespeare sonnets, or Mrs. Fyleman reading Dickens in her Irish English. The refugee girls had to work hard in vegetable garden and kitchen to help keep the large household going - and calm it was not. Both Margaret Fyleman and Sophie Cahn (then nearly sixty) were tremendously powerful, temperamental personalities and there would be great fallings-out, only outdone by their fallings-back-in. Lotte was divided between fascination at her new environment and gnawing homesickness. What was happening to her parents now that war had been declared by Britain on Germany? What was happening to the friends left behind? She had just had time to write reassuring letters about her surprisingly happy landing. And her parents would have been reassured, if a little wrily conscious of her excited absorption in this new world, before the only communication between them became twenty-five-word Red Cross messages.

It was not easy being a young German Jewish refugee in a Britain at war. [2] When internment of all German `enemy aliens` threatened, they had to live within a five mile radius from a police station to which they reported. They even packed their suitcases for the prison camp on the Isle of Man - until Mrs. Fyleman successfully vouched for them all at the local magistrates' tribunal hearing. Thereafter they had to do what was officially classed as war work and Lotte was drafted to a huge laundry. Soon after Dunkirk she was rounded on by her fellow workers as a German enemy; she could not make them understand the difference it made being a German Jew. She was still German, wasn't she? She could only cry. Perhaps Mrs. Fyleman saw Lotte's unhappiness; in any event, her sister, Lady Helen Seymour-Lloyd, was looking for a new lady's maid/companion – and chose Lotte to come and live with her in Oxford. This second transplantation only intensified Lotte's homesickness and her worry about all those she loved in Mainz. Then two things happened. She received the last Red Cross message from her parents, written months earlier, (`THE RED CROSS TELEGRAM`). She could not yet realize the full horror of what it meant but it read like a farewell. Her helpless anxiety deepened. The other event was that a very young man called Fritz Kramer, a fellow refugee, managed, with Sophie Cahn's help, to find Lotte in Oxford. He had once been her school-fellow in Mainz and had first proposed to her when she was twelve. He proposed again. Lotte left

Lady Helen Seymour-Lloyd and Oxford, including her new, precious Adult Education literature classes, and was transplanted for a third time, to live with Fritz in London and work once more in a huge laundry until the war was over.

In May 1945 Lotte was not quite twenty-two. She had heard nothing more from or about her parents for three years. Her desperate searches through the International Red Cross now yielded no more information than that they had last been traced to some village in Poland in 1942. She gave herself to the terrible, long drawn-out attempt to keep on hoping: sometime, somewhere her parents would be found among the millions of 'displaced persons', weak and ill of course, but able to be nursed back to life by her. Finally she stopped hoping. She never learned how or where or when they had been murdered, or whether or not they had been together to the end. In all she lost twelve family members to the Nazi exterminators.

'Unbearable truth' is not just a phrase, it is a fact. It really was unbearable, if she were to stay sane, to imagine the worst over and over again. 'For thirty years/I locked your nameless graves. /I stamped on grief' ('STONE-SETTING'). Lotte Kramer concentrated, as her mother had done before her, on making a home; but in her case she brought up her only child to be safely English. She buried her past until there came a fourth transplantation. Her husband's place of employment changed from

London to Cambridgeshire and she found herself in the late 1970s in Peterborough, where she knew no–one. It was a new period of `unbelonging`. Living alone during the week, she began to think - and her suppressed memories at last came back to life inside her. But what was there to be done with them? How could she fight her mental fight against madness, not just depression but the madness of an implacable, obsessive, all-encompassing hatred of every German?

  Although she had always been a compulsive reader of German and English classical literature (and if the times had been different she too would surely have studied and become a *Gymnasium Studienraetin* for German and English like Sophie Cahn), her formal education had been arrested abruptly when she was fifteen. She did not think it possible either that she could write – or, for that matter, that anyone could write - about the Holocaust.

  "Karen Gershon has done so," the poet Edward Storey told her one day in Peterborough.

When Lotte Kramer read the poems of Karen Gershon, like herself a *Kindertransport* refugee whose parents had been murdered by the Nazis, she realized that it <u>was</u> possible to write about the impact of the Holocaust, but that she herself must write differently. Despite her admiration for Gershon's emotional honesty - `Ahead of me always/You told our black song ` (`DIRGE`, 1994), - Lotte Kramer could not share the other writer's unassuageable bitterness towards all Germans, her

anger at her alien refugee status in England, or her Zionist solution in

Israel. It was not easy for Lotte Kramer to begin to write in the 1970s –

and it was, if anything, even less easy at first to get her poems published.

The earliest memories were imprinted on the mind of a German

schoolgirl, but when the words came, over forty years later, she began to

write in her adoptive English, often unrhymed, ironically aware, hinting

at harmonies:

> *Myself, I'm unsure*
> *In both languages. One with mothering*
> *Genes, at once close and foreign*
> *After much unuse. Near in poetry.*
> *The other a constant love affair*
> *Still unfulfilled, a warm*
> *Shoulder to touch.*
> (BILINGUAL, in <u>The Desecration of Trees</u>, 1994)

Between 1980 and 2007, however, she has published nine collections of

poetry in Britain and one German-English volume in Germany. [3] The

translation into Japanese of a selection of her poems is now being

prepared; many of her poems have been published in poetry magazines

and in poetry anthologies in several different countries. She has been

reviewed very appreciatively in <u>Poetry Review</u>, <u>PN Review</u>, <u>European</u>

<u>Judaism</u>, and <u>The Independent on Sunday</u>, i.a. as well as in <u>The Times</u>

<u>Literary Supplement</u>. The London Underground has published `Exodus`

among its `Poems on the Underground` in 2003 and the BBC has, over the years, broadcast four of her poems, by public request, in its programme `Poetry Please`.

What is so special and important about Lotte Kramer's poetry relating to the Holocaust?

She wastes hardly any time on the perpetrators; her overwhelming concern is to resurrect her humane dead. What helped her above all in her long drawn out struggle not to go mad with hatred were two factors. First, she recognised just how easily she too could have been part of the collective psychosis of Nazism as a brainwashed German child. For had not her ten-year-old self also responded, shining-eyed with the others, to the singing and to all the appeals to idealistic sacrifice for the *Vaterland*? How could she ever be sure that, if she had been nothing but German, she would have grown up brave enough to resist that powerful dictatorship by racist criminals? So how could she judge the non-resisters? And there was a second, even more powerful factor. For the Wertheimers had been blessed, not just with a loyal servant maid and the odd concerned neighbour, but with an extraordinarily deep friendship with a German couple and their daughter, sharing the same apartment house - and Christmas and Channukah and music-making – over many years. The Trempers, Catholic teachers, had had the love and courage to support the Wertheimers to the end, at no matter what fearsome risk to themselves: "To call you faithful would not be enough" (`FRIENDS`). And just as they had borne witness, so Lotte Kramer bears witness to them. One of the most moving poems in this book is the sonnet `POST-WAR V` written to their daughter, Greta Berdolt, Lotte Kramer's dearest friend: `Your letter, searching for me, crossed with mine / Searching for you...` When the Kramers made their first return visit to their native Mainz in the 1950s, it was Greta Berdolt who met them at the railway station.

There are many other people whom Lotte Kramer resurrects. Dead relatives, teachers, Mrs. Fyleman, and above all her own parents, beginning with the time before she knew them or they knew each other in `LOVE LETTERS`. She did not set out to write a careful chronological account of her experience of mid-20th Century European history. On the contrary, she would feel moved in the early 1980s to write about something that had happened in 1937 and in 1987 about something that had happened in 1933 and in 1994 she would jump forward to 1946 and back again to the early thirties. Her most recent poems often link past, present and future and so place her own traumatic German Jewish history within the long history of human inhumanity, universalising it. All her poems that respond to the *Kindertransport* experience and the Holocaust are scattered throughout her various collections which include poems and translations on quite other subjects altogether. I feel, however, that in her own way, Lotte Kramer <u>has</u> been a historian, a quiet inner historian of her time, and therefore I have put her *Kindertransport*, Before and After poems together here for the first time, and arranged them in such a way as to give the sense of a meditation on European history, 1920 - 2007.

Although, as she told me in an interview, "the grief does not get better, it gets worse," Lotte Kramer has waged a heroic mental struggle never to give up on her humanism. In this she reminds one of Irène Némirovsky writing about the young German soldiers in France suddenly ordered to invade Russia: `I swear here and now never again to take out my bitterness, no matter how justifiable, on a group of people, whatever their race, religion, convictions, prejudices, errors. I feel sorry for these poor children. `[4] Euripides warned us in tragedy after tragedy that suffering all too often deforms the sufferer and so initiates the next sequence of righteous cruelty. Lotte Kramer's understated, profoundly felt poems testify that suffering does not <u>have</u> to deform us all until the whole world ends in fire. [5]

Sybil Oldfield, July 2007

Notes.

1. See Sybil Oldfield, `"It Is Usually She": the role of British women in the rescue and care of the *Kindertransport* Kinder`, in Shofar, vol.23, no.1, (Fall 2004).

2. cf. Karen Gershon, We came as Children: A Collective Autobiography of Refugees, (1st. publ. 1966; London, 1989); Bertha Leverton and Shmuel Lowensohn, eds. I Came Alone, the Story of the *Kindertransports*, (Sussex, 1990); and Hanna Behrend, `An Austrian Refugee in Wartime Manchester` in Sybil Oldfield, ed. This Working-Day World, Women's Lives and Culture(s) in Britain 1914-1945, (Taylor and Francis, 1994).

3. Heimweh. Homesick. Gedichte herausgegeben und uebersetzt von Beate Hoerr, (Frankfurt, 1999). In an interview with Beate Hoerr, Lotte Kramer has said that the German Jewish fate is to be homesick all one's life long. Both in an emotional and a literary sense, part of her has remained a German exile. For it was only Hitler and his followers who denied her the possibility of being German and why should she obey them? Her poetry is grounded in German as well as in English lyricism.

4. Irène Némirovsky, Suite Francaise. Chatto and Windus, 2006, Appendix 1, diary note, 28 June, 1941.

5. "My own experience has made me realise that understanding between religions is vital and I have been a longstanding member of the Council

of Christians and Jews, ...I want to promote tolerance and appreciation

... both here and also in Germany. There some young people have shown

great determination in the attempt at reconciliation without forgetting."

(Lotte Kramer, `Reflections, <u>The Jewish Yearbook 2000</u>)

The Poems

Before

*`My ghosts return
Unforgotten`.*

(`SALT`, in <u>Black over Red</u>, 2005)

LOVE LETTERS

Alone at home one afternoon
I found them in my father's desk.
A bolted fortress, as a rule –
But now a drawer yielded,
There they lay, ribboned
And stacked in one elaborate box:
Letters my parents had received
Before their marriage.

Strange sympathy I felt
For that young Christian girl
His mother disapproved of –
For many years her lines
Had burnt and cradled him.
Hers were the only ones he'd kept.

But on my mother's side
A pot-pourri of males:
Some officers in trenches
Shimmering with her praises
Written in muddy misery.
Another she'd made eyes at
From a theatre box;
One, a Black Forest holiday friend
Who even called her 'bride' -

Like pickles they had been preserved
Inside this occult box
Not seeing daylight much,
Not for a daughter's eyes.

(The Desecration of Trees, 1994)

ANECDOTE 1920s, Rhineland

"There wasn't much to eat then"
So she said,
"But space enough, you knew our flat,
Nine rooms,
The Rhine view from the balcony,
And comfortably set.
So after armistice they
Billeted
French officers with us. They whored
And spat
And lived it up, and they brought fleas –
All in my silk salon.
The maids were always pregnant,
Still, that's that. –
One was refined. He sat and talked
And smoked
Long after meals were over. Well,
You know your father's tact,
He would not hurt a fly. All
Sensitive
Benevolence, all justice, law,
Forget,
Forgive old enmities. Don't step
On any Frenchman's toes.
But on that afternoon, that
Officer
Began accusing us – as Bôches –
Of war
Atrocities. In Belgium too!
Your father sat on coal,
How I could sense his fever!
Silently
He rose and only spoke three words:
'Et les Vôtres?'
God, I was terrified. He might
Have gone to jail for that!"

('New Poems' in Selected and New Poems 1980-1997)

ICE-BREAK

Snow and ice have lain
Rich and fat on the grass
For days,
On river and lake the silver
Is sitting as stubborn
As oil,
Each blade and twig has a
Metal skin of its own.

The light cuts right through the years
And I find myself small
By the side
Of my father, quite close to his hand,
Our feet step in careful tread on the ice,
The Rhine
Now a new white street without end,
The reliable river vanished or dead.

Yet alive
With a fun-fair crowd
On its broad, hard chest,
As men
Use the solid water instead of earth
And dancing deny its escape
And birth,
But the poem insists on its flow
With the ice-break of words.

(Ice-break, 1980)

GERMANY 1933

The air was dank with fifty little girls.
Spell-bound they listened to their teacher's tale
Of one young martyr*, one who gave the name
To that new hymn. They wept for him. He burnt

An early hero into ready minds.
And then the oath – they hardly knew what for –
Of loyalty to him whose massive roar
Bludgeoned their ears. There was no choice, no sign

Of something sinister. They longed to serve,
To sing in great processions, hold a flag,
And feel secure under this pagan tag.
A slag-heap waiting for a willing herd.

'Now choose the one to lead, to march ahead,
To keep your trust, unfurl the swastika'
The teacher urged a ballot on the class.
'The one you like the most' he archly said.

The children chose and named a Jewish child

(The Shoemaker's Wife, 1987)

*Horst Wessel

A NEW SUBJECT

'Today we start a subject that is new
To everyone. As your new master now
I've come to tell you something of those true
Great ancestors we have. You must be proud,

You boys, our fatherland, our new decade,
Is nurtured by a giant race: red-blond,
Eyes blue, a strong physique and unafraid.
The finest ethnic heritage is ours.

Let's see the type of man we used to be -
Yes you – just there – behind that darkish head,
You in the seventh row – get up, come here!
What is your name? Ah, Heinz, ah, very good.

Now face the class. You see in this blond boy
The perfect specimen of purest race;
His bones are powerful, his hair is fair,
His eyes are blue set in an eager face.

No shameful mixture in his blood of breed.
This is your future now, our Germany!
You grin – you laugh – you too – I'll have no cheek
From anyone! What is the matter, speak?'

'Please Sir, it makes no sense, it's true, you see
Heinz is a Jew.'

(Earthquake, 1984)

GRANDFATHER

For me
He was the unassailable giant.
The creator of bicycles and dolls,
The law of God behind his butcher's apron

He smelt
Of sausages and fresh air,
And he grew out of his small town
As naturally as a Black Forest pine tree.

Not quite
In tune he would sing to me,
With tears in his voice and eyes,
His well-worn folk-songs and ballads.

His word
Was gospel to his family,
And his wife's large domesticity
Was ornament and shape for his great size.

No one
Dared to correct him.
For him it was right to stub his roll,
To saturate his moustache and napkin,

So when
One April Fool's Day
They barricaded his shop and house,
He, like an angry god, turned away from the living.

(Family Arrivals, 1981)

GRANDMOTHER

She could walk no further
    Than the garden gate,
Her black skirt dusting hot sand;
    Where the yellow heat
Bent down to us as it spanned
    - From a sunflower's face –
Her slowing bones that belied
    Her agile eyes.

In their brightness quickened
    Eighty years of life:
The wisdom of long widowhood;
    The time of briskness;
The stride to the water pump;
    To the bales of cloth
She had wound and unwound like
    Multi-coloured snails.

Her look hunted hardship:
    That barbed-wire gaze
That had governed her five sons
    Still ruled without words
From a filigree frame.
    And the linen she wove
With a sun-shy hand still cools
    And calms my face.

(<u>A Lifelong House</u>, 1983)

THE TABLECLOTH

A tablecloth,
A white, coarse linen weave,
A dead thing, so it seems.
Its threads are gently rent
In places, as in dreams,
When falling into pits
We wake in unbelief.

So frays this weft.
My father's mother made
The cloth in quiet days.
What patient thoughts she wove
Around this loom, narrow
Village ways, important
Hours underlined her shade.

Now, when I touch
This fragile web, and spread
It with our wine and bread,
And watch it slowly die,
I grieve not for its breach
But for the broken peace,
The rootlessness, our dread.

(Family Arrivals, 1981)

9

MY FATHER WAS A WRITER

My father was a writer.
His dusty manuscripts
Were stacked like paper patterns
In corners of the desk.

When young, his plays were living
On stages by the Rhine,
And promises of vision
Traced humour through his time.

I still remember photos:
Surrounded by his cast,
A minor Proust – and almost
A scalpel poised as sharp.

In Kaiser's war-time dodgings
He found Roumania's heat.
There, in a soldier's lodging
He daily stencilled sheets

With finely measured letters
Describing dirt and blood.
He bundled them like treasures
And kept the drawer shut.

"I'll write a tragedy one day"
He used to prophesy.
He never saw his Jericho
After the trumpet's cry.

(Black over Red, 2005)

A DRAMATIST WHO WAS MY FATHER

All day, on Sundays,
He walked in the woods, alone,
Needing exhaustion.

The mushroom silence
Of trees tuned his voice,
The sudden brightness

Of meadows glazed
And bandaged his icon-wounds
Of unwritten words.

At home, old manuscripts
Yellowed and mourned in dense
Drawers of his desk;

But still new lines
That would never smell ink
Or paper breathed

Their last upright
Declensions on a stage-set
Of queues and gas,

His words, now ashes,
Bitter, perpetual powder
On my tongue.

(A Lifelong House, 1983)

11

SCHULS TARASP REVISITED

(for my father)

Dear marching hero, tracing your long strides
Along the boulders of the river Inn
Walking away the demons of your mind,
I feel their tremor on the bridge and run

When crossing to the gorge. You loved that Spa:
The elegance beside the steaming spring,
The promenading while you sipped that raw
And sulphurous drink, the afternoons that cling
To Kurhaus gardens, coffee, schmaltzy dance,

Light years away from hostile marching songs.
They cushioned you, those quiet weeks, the rhythm
Reeking of Edwardian follies and their time
(And yet between two 20th century wars)
When mountains could displace that crooked cross.

No premonition then of that dark curse
That would destroy your summers, seal my loss.

(The Shoemaker's Wife, 1987)

THE NON-EMIGRANT
(my father in Nazi Germany)

He left the application forms
Hidden inside his desk and missed
His quota for the U.S.A.

He thought he'd stay and wait and stare
The madness out. It could not last.
He would not emigrate, not lose

His home, his language and his ground.
Beside his armchair sat a pile
Of books; the smoke from his cigar

Fenced comfort with a yellow screen.
His daily walk was all he'd need,
He thought. Abroad was where he'd been.

(<u>The Desecration of Trees</u>, 1995)

WAVING

'Poor men,' my gentle mother said,
'Let's wave to them, they have no joy!'
And from the train, her frantic arm
Waved to those men in zebra stripes,
The prisoners, hacking at stones.

Some dared return that gestured hope;
A germ, a spark – swift as the train –
That blanches their black, everyday fear
With quick significance of life:
A waving woman and her child.

(<u>Family Arrivals</u>, 1981)

COFFEE GRINDING

Grinding the coffee in my moulinex
The beans explode their old aroma here.
It clears the ashes out of sleep.

My mind returns to kitchens where I played:
I see our maid, broad on a stool, machine
Placed firmly between thighs:

She wheels the scent with comfortable arms
And sings of love in tune to grating knives.
A reassurance grinds.

I am reminded of another scene:
There, in the synagogue my mother stands
All day to fast and pray;

To keep her from a faintness now I bring
Some coffee finely ground, wafting a strength
Into her silent fears.

(The Desecration of Trees, 1994)

LENA, OUR MAID

She anchored all my needs
In her solidity,
A cross pleat on her brow.

Between her household chores
She'd rush with me to school,
Her rough hands square with
love.

Devout, she made me kneel
On crowded pavement slabs
To watch the bishop pass

Under his baldachin
Intoning Latin chant,
The incense cloud above.

At the stone kitchen sink,
Her yeasty body's shrine,
She'd stand and strip-wash clean,

Then outings into town,
To dark room secrecy
Where she collected hope

From a clairvoyant's words
Behind a curtain fall,
Her love-life's counterpoint.

A butcher boy appeared
And many nights they sighed
On mother's lounge settee

While I pretended sleep
Two doors away. She got
Her man and left. I cried.

Her home two basement rooms
Where she would lie in wait
With plates of chips, the food

I loved, spoiling my lunch.
But still I hear her screams
Up in my room, two floors

Above her flat, when she
Gave birth to her huge son
Her second child, she said.

(The Desecration of Trees, 1994)

FUGUE

[for Sophie Cahn]

There was no irony in it,
After their nightfall arrival.
She always came shadowless now.

This time she brought one in his black
Swastika uniform. They ate
As usual at the oak table.

Then, in the yellow light's comfort
The older woman's accurate
Fingers unpinned a stepping fugue.

His words cut that afterglow calm:

'I did not believe that a Jew
Could play Bach like that, I thank you.'

(A Lifelong House, 1983)

17

THE GURU OF GROCERIES

In my grandfather's town,
In a corner shop,
The smell of spices bounced from the walls,

The goods in a jumble
Of tubs and jars
From fresh Sauerkraut to a mêlée of sweets.

We would skip all the way
To be greeted there
By a soft young man in a kosher-white coat:

The guru of groceries;
He ruled his domain
With his silhouette mother in a velvet back room.

Many children from school
Dropped in on their way
For a bag of sweets, a chat and a smile,

Till one day he had gone;
The shutters were down,
The place was as dead as a drowned house.

Only trickling whispers
Explained with much grief
His forbidden love, his fragile sin

With a girl, not a Jew,
Who had stayed too long.
And we never ever saw him again.

('New Poems', in <u>Selected and New Poems</u>, 1997)

18

SOMETHING I HEARD TODAY

Something I heard today
Reminded me of that long corridor,
The polished silence caught behind each face –
I'd never been inside that place before.

Police – Gestapo were
Vocabularies that shared my growing pains,
Familiar yet abstract as names of squares.
But here we sat and stood in wordless queues.

Three generations waiting
In the narrow light that pressed like lockjaw
On our brains.
          My turn. I went into a
Room, beside a table that still seemed to grow,

And someone grabbed my hand
And stained my thumb and fingertips with ink,
And pressed the spiral secrets form the nerves
On paper.
          Something died then, on that desk.

Later when walking home
Through town, I well remember how I felt:
Not the indignity – I minded most –
But that dumb theft with my, too helpless, hand.

(Family Arrivals, 1981)

PREMONITION

Late afternoon
In a darkening room,
A girl alone.

Outside, the streetlamps,
Lakes of shadows
And hollow footsteps.

On her desk her homework,
Additions, fractions,
Clinging to black ink;

She cannot forge
Cohesive answers
As the night collects.

She feels its menace
Invade each space
In prophetic trance,

And terror as huge
As unexplained mountains
Oppress the minutes.

Fears for her mother's
Unusual absence,
Her orphaned lostness

Are tangible omens
In time's reversals
And future nightmares.

(Earthquake and other poems, 1994)

Kristallnacht

`...when they burnt
The temples, when they rent the doors apart...`

(`FRIENDS`, in <u>A Lifelong House</u>, 1983)

10TH NOVEMBER 1938
(after *Kristallnacht*)

You evoke eloquent images,
Spokesmen for the throttled, the fear-bruised,
But you cannot hear the stark dawn-bell
Nor see the meagre groups of children, afraid.

The early, tapped telephone warnings:
'Don't leave the house, the school is burning!'
The furtive attic floor trembling with
Slap-happy sticks that splinter safety and home.

You don't feel my father's hidden tread
In woods while the thicket's cancer grew
Nor his secret return whispering
Family shadows, the vanished ones that day.

You cannot build crosses with your tongue,
So rich and round, for the precision
Of the operation; wear the thorns
Of ice that walk with anonymous ashes

Because the useless shot in Paris
Burst a man's heart – and his mother's also.

(The Desecration of Trees, 1994)

ATTIC

We stored some dusty things up there.
It smelt of mothballs and bare wood,
A spaceless jumble place to hide.
All day we crouched below the sun
Too young to feel the utter fear.
We heard them scream and beat with sticks –
Now they were near –
    a widow's world
Crashed through her glass, old limbless
Porcelain and brass, her table
Torn from her late, careful touching.
We trembled.
    Someone shouted: 'Halt,
Der Fuehrer will das Treiben nicht!' *
And all was quiet. –
    Then my mother
Cooked some food, and we were waiting
For my father's earth-worn footfall
Returning from the darkening trees.

(Family Arrivals, 1981)

* A courageous non-Jewish German teacher intervened to stop the looting – see Lotte Kramer, 'Reflections' in The Jewish Yearbook 2000, p. [70]

DEATH OF A HEADMASTER

A scientist who spoke equations,
Who wanted clarity
With gold-rimmed eyes.

An Arabist,
A language conjurer
With mathematics as his creed.

He led our Jewish school
With fierce humanity
In Nazi Germany.

That night of fire,
Broken glass
And ashes like a hunchback's fall,

Throttled all sense.
A dogma of a lifetime lost,
A splintered alphabet.

They came at dawn to beat and jeer,
His former pupils
From the gentile school

And left him wordless.
Empty, as a bloodless heart,
He opened up the gas,

Left us in desert wind,
Childhood derailed
Like floundering trains.

(The Phantom Lane, 2000)

FOR FRIEDRICH SANDELS

(March 14 1889 - August 5 1984)

...'Immerhin! Mich wird umgeben
Gotteshimmel dort wie hier,
Und als Totenlampen schweben
Nachts die Sterne über mir.'

Heinrich Heine, 'WO?'

I

Today I walked in his flat birth country;
The soil still sandy, the Rhine massive.
Born in that corner of the river's knee
He was rooted in a delta of vines,
Could reach out in safety for mountains and seas,
Know and teach many legends and lives.
His creed was Greece, his voice was German.

He straddled the Kaiser's field-grey years.
Then clarity purged each failed decade.
His oracle told of the blackest sights
Which no one believed, no one would fear
Until his Delphic burden proved true.

II

On the day of the burning school
He came walking towards us,
Face as grey as his flapping coat:

'Children' he said
'Our headmaster is dead.
 His house in splinters,
 His room full of gas.

 They only smashed my records.'

III

He was forest and meadows,
River and Lieder,
Would praise the grace
Of the poem, the word.
The bright spine of language
Brought yeast to his blood.
History moved
As water's kinship
Leading us through
Odyssean journeys.
He taught us to weep
With Antigone's pleading
Where law was compassion,
Was courage and love.

IV

`Weep for his passing,
Sing for his living,
Give thanks for the seed
Of his harvest words.`

V

`Justus`, his nickname, honoured him.
A celebration of his fair concern
For justice, law and discipline.

We could accept his code of decency,
Learn to respect another's private sphere
And all that forms a friend's identity.

Later, when a new country claimed his word
Of different subjects, languages and creeds,
He marched for civil rights among the crowd.

His Europe changed, became a holiday
Where peaks were climbed by cable-cars, not sweat,
And where a boy's Greek grammar made him cry.

Still anxious in his ninth decade
His letters emphasized his mind's great zest
Probing into and through each complex world.

The day the message came that he had died
I spent in making bread, in kneading dough.
His presence in this ritual close at hand.

(The Shoemaker's Wife, 1987)

THE SHOEMAKER'S WIFE

She came to us walking, at night.
Our bundle of mended shoes.
Hot secrets in her shopping bag.

By the door in the hall she stood
And cried. Her autumn hair
Wild from the wind.

Her red-blue eyes like
Sores in her face,
Sad postmarks

From the cobblers' shop
In the narrow old town
Where her husband hammered

And stitched his days;
Where the sign 'No Jews'
Newly pinned to the door

Pleased her sons'
Keen suspicion
That mastered all our lives.

(The Shoemaker's Wife, 1987)

FRIENDS

To call you faithful would not be enough.
You came at night because the laws were wild
With hate. It could have meant a broken, rough
Diminished life for you and for your child;

It could have been your end. But when they burnt
The temples, when they rent the doors apart
That held our coffined world, when they interned
And chained the silent men and many hearts

Translated fear to death, you found the way
To us. Even before the cattle-trucks
Ordained a new stage of the cross, that day,
Your comfort marked a constancy. It brushed

All bitterness away I might have clutched
At a distorting mask. With love you judged.

(A Lifelong House, 1983)

29

ESCAPE

`...And war was somewhere else.`

(`OXFORD, 1940s` from <u>The Desecration of Trees,</u> 1994)

SUITCASE

Grey and tattered it stands in the attic
Having accomplished sixty odd years
Of survival and childhood memories,
Stuffed tight with mother love and heartache,

Unable to forget the packed trains
Of ownerless children and platforms of tears
Its pock-marked skin a testimony
And emblem of such histories.

What now in this war-world of cul-de-sac lives,
Seekers of all ages for a place to own
Confronting friendlessness in a strange town,
A suitcase, perhaps, of unhappy souls

To be stored in some future eventual attic
Or dumped in a museum as showpiece of luck.

(<u>Black over Red</u>, 2005)

AN OLD PERSIAN RUG

Now getting threadbare, fringeless,
But still a fabled garden
With silky blue reflections
Telling of my father's shoes,
His driven restlessness,
His huge mahogany desk,
His sacred study – a child's
Unbidden mystery
Surrounding him.

Packed in the bottom of my case
To cross the Channel with,
Under the necessary clothes,
The few belongings, photos
That were mine to take:
Some concrete souvenirs.
And it has travelled well,
Its beauty still intact
Caressing my eyes.

(Black over Red, 2005)

ODE TO MARGARET FYLEMAN
who met our *Kindertransport*

She met us in a grim-grey station
And warmth spilled from her eyes,
A light on that smoke-filled morning:
Surrounded and spread from her side.

Her Irish voice was melodious,
Her exuberance infected us all,
She could love and hate profoundly
And her temperament held us in thrall.

There was space for us in her house,
Quite bohemian in every way,
And she cooked huge meals on her kitchen range
In a slap-dash manner each day.

We all flocked to her for protection,
Refugees from life and war,
And her Schubert songs and her Dickens
Filled our evenings by the fire.

So this ode to her and her memory
For the life of art she shared
With a generous heart and gesture
That lives on and defies the world.

(Acumen Magazine, January 2006)

ARRIVAL

When I arrived
The gate was always open,
Broad and unhinged,
The gravel underfoot
Pale apricot,
And in the house itself
The air was bright
At first. A generous
Untidiness
Past sideboards, chairs,
And tables where
So many hands had met,
Until a step, a stair, led
Unexpectedly
Into a darkness which the day
Could never sear:
Those anterooms, mysterious
Passages,
The storing corners by
A spiral stair
Held more than dust. For years
I smelt and saw them
Only in disguise.

So here was England:
By the fire-place,
The tea with scones and soda-bread,
The Irish voice
That read from Dickens, made
Him live for us;
The passion in each breath,
Her Schubert songs!
The shabby, shaking figure
Who was once an
Indian Army Colonel,
Now absorbed in roses, lawns,
And the same curry every week.
A portrait hung
Large, on her study wall:
A grandmother
From Java – beautiful
And like the rest:
A contradiction
Of this island universe.
And not one door was ever locked.

(The Shoemaker's Wife, 1987)

MEMOIR
(for Sophie Cahn)

On certain days
There would appear a photograph:
A young and handsome officer,
Austro-Hungarian, on her desk.
          'The one I should have married'
She explained ' he fell in the Great War.'
And next to him herself,
A soul-struck girl with eyes of coal.

At other times
A former pupil took his place:
A Leonardo face, lost to her now
In war-anaemic Hertfordshire
Here, she worked hard at living
On the land, at keeping rabbits,
Pigs, at unforgetting.
Her hands were sick with unborn music.

(The Shoemaker's Wife, 1987)

EQUATION

As a child I began
To fear the word "Jew"
Ears were too sensitive.
That heritage was
Almost a burden.

Then broke the years of war
In a strange country.
This time they sneered at me
"German" as blemish,
And sealed a balance.

(A Lifelong House, 1983)

OXFORD, 1940s

Then I was "Mother's Help – Lady's Companion",
A teen-age girl in love with fantasies
Walking the wartime Oxford streets and lanes.

The colleges were locked facades to me
Quite out of bounds with military use
But still regarded with romantic awe

As territories one day to be explored
By one who'd shed the enemy alien skin.
Meanwhile there were the books – some treasured

Second-hand, picked up at Blackwell's for a song.
An early Schnitzler with the spine in shreds
And hinted sex in dashes worming through

To savour secretly. Before permissiveness.
Long, lonely afternoons up Shotover,
The hill that took me past an empty church

I sometimes entered, praying in my search
For something new and weatherproof
But never found. Years looking for a clue.

A cleric gave a lecture, gaunt, severe,
On faith, a Puritan of sorts, a Scot
Who sent me down a draughty corridor

A mile or two. Not very far, 'Macbeth'
Came to the theatre and filled my head,
My bones and bloodstream ever since, the breath

Of witches stoking up my words. A flame
As permanent as air. And British
Restaurants would earn their wholesome name

With calories that lined my ribs. U.S.
Canteens were treasure troves that sometimes
Spilled their gems. And war was somewhere else.

(The Desecration of Trees, 1994)

38

MEANWHILE

'What do we know of nights in cattle-trucks ...?'

('DEPORTATION' in <u>Family Arrivals</u>, 1981)

'...Of those who suffered not in beds
Who had to queue for death.'

('SOME KINDS OF PAIN' in <u>Ice- break</u>,1980)

Deutsches Rotes Kreuz
Präsidium / Auslandsdienst
Berlin SW 61, Blücherplatz 2

- 7.APR.1942 * 2S0...

ANTRAG
an die *Agence Centrale des Prisonniers de Guerre, Genf*
— Internationales Komitee vom Roten Kreuz —
auf Nachrichtenvermittlung

REQUÊTE
de la Croix-Rouge Allemande, Présidence, Service Etranger
à l'Agence Centrale des Prisonniers de Guerre, Genève
— Comité International de la Croix-Rouge —
concernant la correspondance

1. Absender *Ernst Israel Wertheimer*
   Expéditeur *Mainz/Rhein Taunusstr 45 I*

bittet, an
prie de bien vouloir faire parvenir à

2. Empfänger *Lotte Wertheimer C/o Mrs Mc*
   Destinataire *Egleman Irnig Herts (England)*
   Sendley House

folgendes zu übermitteln / *ce qui suit :*

(Höchstzahl 25 Worte!)
(*25 mots au plus!*)

Unser Wohnsitz ändert sich
Alles Gute, bleibe gesund geliebtes Kind
Gottes Segen wird mit Dir sein. Küssen
Dich In Liebe gedenken Dir immer
Deine Eltern

(Datum / *date*)
20.3.42

(Unterschrift / *Signature*)
Ernst Israel Wertheimer
Lotte Sara Wertheimer

3. Empfänger antwortet umseitig
   Destinataire répond au verso

40

THE RED CROSS TELEGRAM

The red-cross telegram
Read when it came
Those five and twenty words;
The terror, fear,
Was there; I did not dare
To grasp the cruelty
That now I know
It did contain:
'We have to move,
Our residence will not
Remain this town,
Farewell, beloved child.'
How can I ever sing
A requiem
In silent, dark despair,
Transfiguring
Your calvary of nails
And gas and graves.

(<u>Family Arrivals</u>, 1981)

ON SHUTTING THE DOOR

Often, when I leave home,
I think of you,
How you'd have shut the door
That last time
They fetched you out at dawn.

What fears would prophesy,
What intimations
Could foretell the terrors
Of those plains,
The herding into ash?

Or maybe, you looked round
As if before
A holiday, leaving
No trace of dust
No crumbs for pests, no moths

In cupboards, carpets;
Covered the chairs
The settee from the glare
Of light and sun,
Turned off the water, gas…

(The Shoemaker's Wife, 1987)

DEPORTATION

What do we know of nights in cattle-trucks,
Of fires dying on a wire fence,
Of their despair,
Or their release in fumes,

Of their suspended sentence, freezing stance,
And hunger in the ruins of their flesh,
Or of their souls,
Could they still hear the chant?

Some days the lash tears at my skin and bones.
What right have I to soak defeat in fears,
Wet with my tears
My well-fed, balanced face?

I want to lie with them in unknown graves
And bury freedom of indulgent years.
There is no judge
To hear and end their cause.

(Family Arrivals, 1981)

43

RECORDER

In a drawer it rests
Now unplayed,
Chestnut-grained wood;
Many years ago
In another life,
My first musical
Instrument
Evoking a simple tune
With lizard fingers,
The music teacher's
Patient imprint
On my receptive self,
Leading to the more ample
Sound of the piano.
Yet persisting in the lone
Flute-like lament,
Silently unheard
For her whose life was shattered *.

(Agenda, 2007)

*Her career was ended as a musicologist by Nazi race laws.

'ES MUSS SEIN'
[Beethoven Quartet motif]

She bit her wrists
Until the blood was flowing,
Then sank down deeper
In the crowd,
The fetid truck,
And waited for the notes
Inside her mind
To sing
     'It has to be.'*

(The Phantom Lane, 2000)

*The music-teacher of `Recorder` killed herself during deportation.

A GLASS OF WATER

Stands there, in front of you
While you turn the pages,
You look up and see through

That clearness into their
Hearsay world, the heat,
The stench, you could not share

In Poland's cattle-trucks.
The old imaginings:
Hands that beseech and pluck

At air for charity
From somewhere, water most
Of all. Your lips are dry.

You reach out for the glass
But falter, cannot drink.
A feeble gesture, this,

No help to them to let
Your thirst be paramount.
And still you cannot lift

That water to your mouth.
This afternoon you sip
Saliva, feed on breath,

Know the necessity
Of useless obsequies
In solidarity

With shadows that will stay
Beyond this glass of water's
Living chemistry.

('New Poems' in <u>Selected and New Poems</u>, 1987)

QUICKSAND

There must have been
A waiting in the air,
A sort of dying
We know nothing of.
Not like a war,
A combat, a quick kill,
No tooth for tooth
But quicksand in the wind.

Some stood at praying
On Atonement Day
And swayed with vows:
'Kol Nidrei Adonai'
When that feared whisper crept
Below their chant
They dropped their prayer-shawl
And slowly went.

(Black over Red, 2005)

Unbearable Truth

`That time
When the `Final Solution`
Became known as the unacceptable fact...`

(`A FABLE` in <u>Earthquake</u>, 1994)

49

POST-WAR II

Then I'd rush home at night and look for mail
From Europe, via the Red Cross, maybe,
To say my parents had been traced, though frail
And ill but still alive…a dream for me

And many others. A sterile make-belief
That led to nightmares, split my mind. The days
Were filled with slogging work. I buried grief,
Hunted for rations, joined banana queues.

Now looking back from years they never reached
I wonder who she was, this person 'I'
Who rushed up the bare stair-boards that we shared

With other tenants in the house. I try
Pursuing her into our two-room flat
And will not find that letter on the mat.

(<u>Earthquake</u>, 1994)

POST-WAR IV

Then came the news from France of who'd survived
From all the family. Just one or two
By a mere thread of miracle returned
From hell to shadow those whose names caused too

Much pain remembering. And when we met
Again for the first time, below the joy
Were tales untold or only hinted at.
They'd walked on quicksand through a human lie.

We could not know a fraction of their fears.
Our trauma had been statelessness and war
That branded us as aliens in those years
When we were allies really from before

Hostilities. Our lives could not compare
With those dark memories that they could not share.

(Earthquake, 1994)

51

POST-WAR V

Your letter, searching for me, crossed with mine
Searching for you. My 'Wahlverwandtschaft' * older
Sister in enemy country. Not one sign
Of bitterness. Knowing of bombs and fire

Where we used to play and fearing for your
Life so many times, to see your writing
On the envelope crossed grief with joy. For
Now you told me how you fled still carting

Those mementos that my mother brought at dawn,
Her curfew visits, how you saved your child,
Your mother too. But war had meant destruction
Of our town, and worst: had felled your husband.

In those first letters we nailed down our tales
Of you as widow, I as orphan, balanced scales.

(Earthquake, 1994)

Wahlverwandtschaft = kindred spirit

52

NEIGHBOURS 1942-43

So this was how they went:
With layers of clothes
Prepared for ice.
Some gems and coins
Sown into hems,
Perhaps to help escape.

You came the night before
To stem their dark.
To lay your words
On open souls
And bind with hands
A will to outlive hell.

But when your husband fell
In Warsaw's fight,
Left fatherless
Your child – quite close
To him they lost
That breath that willed my life.

(The Shoemaker's Wife, 1987)

LAMENT AND CELEBRATION
i.m. Greta Berdolt

You now
Under a blanket of flowers
Diminish
My childhood's mirror:

Though I stood
In the yard of the old house
Looking up
To your terrace of summer,
Your voice
Of Schubert's *'Lindenbaum'*
Cutting the bark
Of the afternoon's quiet;
I have walked
Past wine-soaked cellars
Hearing the organ
You played in St. Stefan's.

At nightfall
You taught me to see

Fairytale castles
In the fire's landscape;
Midsummer
In a midnight park
You showed me
Pin-lights of glow-worms.
Through streets of terror
You came as night's shadow
Giving new names
To courage and love.

Again the heat
In the leafstill forest,
The dominant river
We can swim in no longer.
Your presence
In your garden's coolness,
A roof of trees
In secret corners
After the spade's earthfall.

(The Desecration of Trees, 1994)

A FABLE

That time
When the `Final Solution`
Became known as the unacceptable fact

You sat
In front of me on an English bus:
The back of your head, your hair, your skin,

The way
The nape of your neck with its small
Dark point moved from side to side

In cautious
Rhythm, the slightly helpless
Expression of your thin shoulders ...

The shock
Shivered through me like fire.
Seconds of fabled seeing until

The other
Woman with the stranger's face
Turned round to get off at the next stop.

(Earthquake, 1994)

SALT

Am I
Like Lot's wife
Having looked at Sodom
Now silenced
To a salt pillar
Without words?

My ghosts return
Unforgotten.

(Black over Red, 2005)

PAST, PRESENT, FUTURE

`I share my scars /With each young orphan's wound. `

(`STONE-SETTING` in <u>Family Arrivals</u>, 1981)

FAMILY ARRIVALS

There is the same excitement at their coming,
Here, where the ballet of the airport shudders;
I feel the forecast of their certain summer.

A generation past I saw the shunting
Of steam and wheels as backcloth to arrivals,
And sensed the fever in my mother's waiting.

For them the hours of travelling are the same;
Though continents and destinations change,
Their shoulders rounder and their walking slow,

They bring their love now in transparent hands.
In pain we cross a platform of a past
And see the missing ones we dare not name.

(<u>Family Arrivals</u>, 1981)

FINAL SOLUTION

They've been mowing down the wild grasses,
And the camomile in the lane
Is buried under black tarmac;
Its scent used to rise to my brain
And remind me of tea that my mother
Was brewing to soothe away pain.

And they, who were cutting the grasses
And stifling the weed in the lane,
Did they care for the shape of a flower,
Did they know of the herb for the pain?

And they, who had ordered the killing
On well-polished telephones –
Was it easy when men are so willing
To diminish each other like stones?

(<u>Ice-break</u>, 1980)

STONE-SETTING

For thirty years
I locked your nameless graves.
I stamped on grief
When it assumed the days
And hid the dark
That slept inside my brain.

I could not speak
Of you. But you were here:
Deep, in my son's
Known eyes, in fisted streets,
On mountain's glass,
And in a valley's heat.

Like you, I felt
That river bleed through me.
Now I unbolt
Your earth, try to incise
On gravestone's bark
My words of branching peace.

I share my scars
With each young orphan's wound,
And man's blind guilt.

(<u>Family Arrivals</u>, 1981)

BARRICADES

She is wailing in the archaic
German of her childhood
Across continents of cinders
Unthought of by doctors and nurses

In her long-ago house
She sends us down to the cellar
Through a coal-dark door
To fetch a bottle of lemonade.

She is waiting with certainty
For her dear husband's arrival
But weeps because 'too many
Stones on the path –
                        he can't cross the stones.'

Her room is my prison.
My shame is my fear
Of her plundered world
I refuse to enter.

(The Desecration of Trees, 1994)

THE LADDER

Today she came,
The lady of good works,
To talk of faith
Behind her coffee cup,
To strum the keys
Of her utopian chord.

"They did not die in vain,
those children in the cattle trucks,
You'll see their spirit rise
And gather peace throughout the world."

And goodness shone like butter
On her face and oiled
Her hot-line ladder to the sky
And who am I
Here, on the lowest rung?

(The Desecration of Trees, 1994)

JUDGEMENT

You, who have not walked
Through the blurred edge of my Hades,
Who have never been dwarfed
By insisting clinkers of spent flames,
Who look not for a name
In anonymous ashes –
Do not encapsulate
A judgement or eavesdrop on pain,
But learn to move
In the flux of a stranger's veins
Over mountains
And from room to room.

(<u>Earthquake</u>, 1994)

KADDISH

Thirty years on:
The wall unbricks itself
And look by look a childhood's
Rawness stands and turns:
"Confront me Now!"

Forty years on:
The named, the nameless queue
And walk their histories,
Demand a chronicle:
"Remember us!"

Fifty years on:
Not late, not loud, the trumpet
Weeps this jubilee,
The skeletons return:
Sad hieroglyphs.

(The Desecration of Trees, 1994)

KINDERTRANSPORT REUNION

A doddery crowd with the same history,
We hug shoulders and clasp hands,
Weeping, laughing at new nearness.

The same faces with stencilled age
We are survivors of circles of hell
Having slid through some six decades

With the usual joys and losses as shadows,
Able to look back at spontaneous goodness
That has confronted our sceptical childhood.

Whereto now as a new century
Is taking hold with much talk
And almost indecent heralding haste?

Begin again in wonder at the brain's
Possibilities, stare at the lilac's candles
Renewing their perfume each spring.

(The Phantom Lane, 2000)

SUBJUNCTIVE

I wonder, had you lived
Into my married years,
Become a grandmother,
A mother-in-law,
Would we have stayed
As closely bound?

Would you have understood
My terrors, doubts,
The years of searching,
Feeling my way
For yet another thought,
Another creed, perhaps?

Would you've been tolerant
Of my rejection of the old
Considered insufficient then,
Or turned away in grief,
Been disappointed
In your daughter's treason?

Would I have run to you
When lifelines changed
Love to a spider's web,
Or kept it hidden
In my ghetto's night
Afraid to burden you?

(The Phantom Lane, 2000)

SOMETIMES

Sometimes
When I can cross the pain,
I find your azure certainty,
Your smiling gentleness:

       Your shopping net
       A careless balance
       To the afternoon.
       You meet my schoolday stream
       With kneading hands of bread.

On other days
Your face is thin as gauze.
Your uncombed hair,
Your searching hands
Awake with fissured skin
Deforming loneliness to fear.

(<u>Black over Red</u>, 2005)

THE SOUND OF ROOTS

You remember more each day
Of language, people and town.
You have returned, a long way
From the burdened child to this sound

Of the whispering roots: "Come near",
They say, "Shed your fear, turn your
Janus head and see how far
And deep we can stretch through the years

Through the centuries in this soil.
We moved with the Rhine, knew the Roman
Yoke, the crusaders' cruel toil.
Yet we harbour here where wine

Grows strong, where we still belong,
Do you hear?" Yes, you listen
And let the blindfold fall from
Your stranger's eyes and you mourn.

(<u>Earthquake</u>, 1994)

HOMESICK

Still the same search for home.
Not a return,
Nor familiarity,
But the once-known
Threshold of otherness.

Years wipe away
Your fingermarks. Your chair
Is too clean; too
Much light waits in this room;
These curtains fall

Together pointlessly.
Other voices
Carpet the stairs, picture
A wall, a nail
Curls against their colours,

Breaks inside me.
I must look for a place
Without echoes:
Hope will breed in a bed
Of hopelessness.

(Earthquake, 1994)

69

DREAMS

You asked me: "Do you dream?"
Too quickly I agreed.
But then pleaded forgetfulness.

Because there is ruthlessness in dreams:
I see the queues of death,
Their last relentless walk.

I run and run and run
But never reach them.
Then I fall.

Sometimes you stand there
In the distance,
Arms apart.

Again I run
Into that lean, far light,
But fall outside myself.

(<u>The Shoemaker's Wife</u>, 1987)

THE SLEEPING BOW-TIE

A crocheted bow-tie
Sleeps in my chest of drawers.

My mother made it
In quiet days.

It has never been worn,
A useless piece

And yet I cannot
Discard it.

Sleep on, sleep on,
Join her ashes

From a long way off
Together with mine.

(The Interpreter's House (magazine), October 2006)

EXODUS

For all mothers in anguish
Pushing out their babies
In a small basket

To let the river cradle them
And kind hands find
And nurture them

Providing safety
In a hostile world:
Our constant gratitude.

As in this last century
The crowded trains
Taking us away from home

Became our baby baskets
Rattling to foreign parts
Our exodus from death.

(<u>Black over Red</u>, 2005)

Lotte Kramer's Publications

*Ice-Break, Annakinn, Peterborough, 1980.

*Family Arrivals, Poet and Printer, London, 1981 and 1992.

*A Lifelong House, Hippopotamus Press, Frome, 1983.

*The Shoe-maker's Wife, Hippopotamus Press, Frome, 1987.

The Desecration of Trees, Hippopotamus Press, Frome, 1994.

Earthquake and other poems, Rockingham Press, Ware, Herts., 1994.

Selected and New Poems 1980-1997, Rockingham Press, Ware, Herts.,

1997 & 2005.

Heimweh. Homesick, ed. Beate Hoerr, Brandes & Apsel, Frankfurt a.

Main, 1999.

The Phantom Lane, Rockingham Press, Ware, Herts., 2000.

`Reflections`, in The Jewish Yearbook 2000, London, p. [69] – p. [75].

Black over Red, Rockingham Press, Ware, Herts., 2005.

Kindertransport, Before and After: Elegy and Celebration, Centre for

German Jewish Studies, University of Sussex, 2007.

-----

* Out of print

Check-list of the critical reception of Lotte Kramer's poetry.

1981, PN Review, (Dick Davis)

Summer 1984 Agenda, (Karen Andrews).

1985, The Jewish Quarterly.

Summer, 1987, Agenda. (Edward Lowbury).

Autumn-Winter 1994/5, Agenda, (Kathleen Raine).

Spring 1998, European Judaism, (George Szirtes).

5 June, 1998, The Times Literary Supplement, (Janet Montefiore).

Winter 1998/9, Poetry Review, (Gillian Allnutt).

2000, Other Poetry, (Anne Stevenson).

September 2001, Acumen.

2002, AJR (Association of Jewish Refugees).

2003, European Judaism, (Shirley Toulson).

2005, Common Ground, Council for Christians and Jews, (Edward Storey)

September, 2005, Acumen.

2005, AJR, (Association of Jewish Refugees).

2005, Ambit.

January 2006, Jewish Renaissance.

17 February, 2006, Jewish Chronicle.

February/March 2006, The London Magazine.

2007, John Clare Society Journal, Nottingham Trent University.